Guide to the C-Suite of Fast-growing Companies

Contents

Essential Skills in a Fast-growing Company's CEO 4

Skills in Entrepreneurs versus Skills in C-Suite Executives 7

Launching New Products in Fast-growing Companies 12

Scaling up to an Effective Organizational Culture 18

Improving the Cash Flow of a Fast Growing Company 22

Improving the Profitability of a Fast-growing company 26

Market Positioning and Market Share in Fast-growing Companies 30

Portfolio Management of Products and Businesses 34

Corporate Governance in For-Profit Companies 38

Corporate Image of an Exit Stage Company 42

Valuation in an Exit Stage Company 47

Pre-IPO Task List 52

About the Author 57

Essential Skills in a Fast-growing Company's CEO

What do Venture Capitalists and Boards look for when they hire a new CEO? Some look for a visionary, whereas some look for a fundraiser, or team leader, or salesperson, or orchestrator, or brand name. The incoming CEO has to be experienced with the leadership, team building, strategy, vision, growth, finance, operations, technology, and culture aspects of the business. Industry experience is helpful. The main goal of a corporation is to increase shareholder (private or public) value, and the CEO has to be exceptionally good with raising money, setting expectations, and exceeding expectations. He/she has to set sight on a distant destination and sail the ship towards it, overcoming all obstacles, with the harmonious support of his/her team.

The basic skills required for all C-suite executives are: Leadership, Strategic

Thinking and Execution, Technical and Technology, Team-and-relationship Building, Communication and Presentation, Change Management, and Integrity. It is unacceptable if the CEO cannot inspire and motivate others, display a high level of integrity, analyze issues and solve problems, drive for results, delegate, communicate effectively, collaborate, and build relationships. The goal is to increase revenues rapidly while keeping all stakeholders engaged, and by setting unprecedented standards for the corporation. It is beneficial if the new CEO is creative, risk-taking, hardworking, and has fundamental management skills.

VCs, boards and search committees will always put credence in analyzing track records and relevant experience, reviewing written reports, and talking to references. But it is in the interview where chemistry is established and essential intangibles like passion, energy, and fit are determined. They have a scorecard for determining the job's mission, the outcomes desired, and the competencies required in the CEO candidate. They press for thorough, descriptive and focused answers to their questions, presenting problems specific to the corporation, and seeking solutions and examples from the candidate's past experiences. Once they have found the right CEO candidate, they sell him/her on fit, freedom and fortune.

Skills in Entrepreneurs versus Skills in C-Suite Executives

Top 7 Skills Entrepreneurs Need

1. **Mental Capabilities**
   Companies like Google, Facebook and Microsoft were started by people with excellent mental capabilities. Depending on the nature of the business and the level of success desired, different levels of mental capabilities are required in an entrepreneur. The average entrepreneur has pretty good mental capabilities.

2. **Optimism**
   Entrepreneurs always see the light at the end of the tunnel. They dig up new tunnels to find the light. They "feel" they can grow their business, achieve enormous financial gain, and increase stakeholder value.

3. **Perseverance**
Entrepreneurs almost never give up. They prefer to experiment and fail, rather than never try. They are very good with following through on, and executing their plans. They are focused on the right goals.

4. **Leadership**
Entrepreneurs often have an evangelistic quality. They have great ideas, and are skilled at getting buy-in from investors and employees. They lead the right people at the right time to attain the right goals. They are often visionaries.

5. **Risk Taking**
Entrepreneurs often seem more comfortable with risk than other business leaders. This can lead to failures, but also stunning successes. The risks that entrepreneurs take are calculated, and aren't simply done for the thrill.

6. **Creative Thinking**
   Entrepreneurs are known for thinking outside the box. They see connections and possibilities where others do not. They have an incredible ability to associate, and they solve problems creatively.

7. **Strong Work Ethic**
   A lot of hard work is required to launch something new. To be successful, entrepreneurs must execute. Entrepreneurs are relentless when it comes to completing projects and following through on the work required to turn ideas and plans into a successful company.

Whether the founders continue being part of the company's leadership team or not, is a decision of the board of directors and investors. As the company grows, some of the founders stay on as C-Suite executives, whereas the others leave, or are demoted. The ones that stay on as C-Suite executives display the following skills:

- Leadership
- Strategic Thinking and Execution
- Technical and Technology Skills
- Team and Relationship Building
- Communication and Presentation
- Change Management
- Integrity

As you can see from the above 2 lists, the skills and traits in a founder are somewhat different than those in a C-Suite Executive. There are many examples of entrepreneurs who have all 14 skills, and who successfully transition from being founders to C-Suite executives. There are also many examples of founders who do not want to relinquish their core professional strengths, and who would rather move on to newer ventures than to become successful C-Suite Executives.

Launching New Products in Fast-growing Companies

You are a fast-growing company, and you already have some products generating revenue. Now, you want to figure out if, when and how you should launch new products. The person who owns the product development process is responsible for taking the product from concept to market.

The first deciding factor for a company to launch a new product or service is to understand whether it has team members who have the right experience, knowledge and skills to concept-test, design and manufacture the same. The next factor is to determine the marketing and promotion strategies. After sales service is something which should never be ignored.

Your employees may have a lot of ideas for launching new products or services. You can evaluate their ideas using the following criteria:

- the customer needs or desires
- the benefits to your target market
- the fit with your current range of product/service offerings
- the fit with your business profile and strategic plans
- the regulatory framework within which it will operate
- the technical feasibility of the idea
- the level and scope of research and development required
- search of patent and other inventor databases
- where the product fits in the market. How close is it to competitor products?
- the profitability of the idea. What is its potential appeal to the market? How would you price it? What are the costs in bringing it to market?
- the marketing potential of the idea

- the resources it will require in development
- where you will get the investment funds for the project
- the timeline with target dates and milestones
- how you will phase the project and control costs

You must examine the status quo of your company and your business objectives before you begin the product development process. Some of the questions to answer are as follows:

1. What corporate strengths can you exploit to produce your product/service?
2. What are your technological capabilities?
3. What are your sales force capabilities?
4. What is your company's current cash/credit position?

5. What is your company known for?
6. Do you prefer to operate in a particular industry?
7. Do you prefer a product sold to retail users, industrial users, government, etc.?
8. Do you prefer a product with a long usage or would you consider a fad item?
9. Do you have a distribution preference?
10. Do you want to distribute internationally?
11. Are you willing to create a new sales and marketing team to support the product?
12. What is the sales volume you expect?
13. Do you have any pricing expectations?
14. Would this product need to be self-sustaining?
15. Does the product need to be internally produced?
16. Would you consider licensing?

17. Would you joint venture with another company for a new product?
18. Are there any physical limitations to the new product or service?
19. Are there any operational limitations?
20. Do you have personnel trained to support the new product?
21. Have you established a budget?
22. Has a timeline been set for when the new product must be profitable?
23. What kind of profit margin is expected?
24. Can the product have seasonal cycles?

Once the development process is complete, you can focus on marketing, selling and scaling. Make sure you delight your customers. Establish a continuous improvement program for launching new products and for your company's new product development process. The objective of introducing a new product in the market is to increase revenues.

Scaling up to an Effective Organizational Culture

Now that you are trying to maintain an innovative culture within your company, you, as a leader, have to watch your behavior. Culture includes the company's vision, values, norms, systems, symbols, language, behaviors, assumptions, beliefs, and habits.

Fast-growing companies can derive the following benefits by developing an effective culture:

- Better alignment of the company towards achieving its vision, mission, and goals
- High employee motivation, loyalty, engagement and effectiveness
- Increased team cohesiveness among the company's various departments and divisions
- Consistency, coordination and control within the company

- Increased efficiency caused by shaping employee behaviors

There are a number of elements that can be used to describe or influence your company's culture:

- The paradigm: What the company is about, what it does, its mission, its values.
- Control systems: The processes in place to monitor what is going on. Role cultures would have vast rulebooks. There would be more reliance on individualism in a power culture.
- Organizational structures: Reporting lines, hierarchies, and the way that work flows through the business. These include accountability charts with key performance indicators, and Profit and Loss and Balance Sheet outcomes.

- Power structures: Who makes the decisions, how widely spread is power, and on what is it based?
- Symbols: These include company logos and designs, but also extend to symbols of power such as parking spaces and executive washrooms.
- Rituals and routines: Management meetings, board reports and so on may become more habitual than necessary.
- Stories and myths: build up about people and events, and convey a message about what is valued within the company.

Cultural Change

In order to make a cultural change effective a clear vision of the company's new strategy, shared values and behaviors is needed. The behavior of the management needs to symbolize the kinds of values and behaviors that should be realized in the rest of the company. The next step is to identify what current systems, policies, procedures and rules need to be changed in order to align with the new values and desired culture. This may include a change to accountability systems, compensation, benefits and reward structures, and recruitment and retention programs to better align with the new values and to send a clear message to employees that the old system and culture are in the past.

An aligned culture will support and facilitate the capabilities needed to achieve strategic goals, whereas a divergent culture will undermine them. Employees with a high level of engagement will "go the extra mile" to reach goals. Employee engagement is measured in terms of ambition, accountability, inspiration, pride, and support. The environment of a company is the main driver of employee behavior. Therefore all leadership behaviors, policies, organization design, and hiring practices should be aligned to achieve the desired culture.

Improving the Cash Flow of a Fast Growing Company

The basic principles of managing cash flow are:

1. Collect more of what you are owed.
2. Collect faster.
3. Maintain timely and accurate financials.
4. Stabilize income and expenses so that they are more predictable and consistent.
5. Sharply manage your expenses.
6. Relentlessly manage and improve your margins.
7. Make smart strategic decisions on purchasing and pricing.

Sources to fund your growth:

1. Customers – Redesign your collections system so that you get

paid up front, charge a premium for enhanced products and services, offer discounts for prepayment, increase your pricing, factoring invoices, purchase order financing, deposits for large orders, extra payments for enhancements, penalize late payers or non-payers, subscription sales method, market segmentation, etc.
2. Vendors – Increase your line of credit, barter with them, build strategic partnerships, stage payments to your benefit, etc.
3. Internal – Build up capital reserves, speed up your production cycle, reduce your collections cycle, reduce your sales cycle, use higher interest earning accounts, sell excess equipment/inventory, accounts receivables line of credit, inventory line of credit, renegotiate fixed debts

to your benefit, delay expansion plans, reduce wages, etc.
4. Investors – Maintain a good track record, calculate the valuation of your company, raise smart money, sell your story, etc.

In order to reduce your Cash Conversion Cycle (for every dollar spent by the company to make its way back into the company), you can shorten individual cycle times, eliminate mistakes, improve the Profit and Loss statement, and/or improve the business model. You can do this for your sales, make/production, inventory, delivery, and billing and payment cycles. You can increase the price, volume and creditor days, or you can reduce cost of goods sold, overheads, debtors' days and stock days.

To maintain rapid growth, the company must balance sales growth with positive

cash flow. In the absence of significant cash flow from financing activities, the key measure is the cash flow from operations. But as we see in most rapidly growing private companies, the company cannot sustain itself without the next round of funding from venture capital or private equity investors. An IPO or an M&A is an option for raising funding only if the company has a worthy track record and growth prospects.

Many cash flow problems are a result of rapid, unpredictable growth. Have a rolling 12-month forecast for cash flow, and if it is a problem, make it one of the top priorities for all employees. Focus on sales, and improving margins through proper market segmentation and pricing strategies. Focus on raising your next round of funding. Whatever you do, don't run out of cash.

Improving the Profitability of a Fast-growing company

It looks like your revenues are growing rapidly, and you are scaling at warp speed. Now you have to set some profitability objectives, which you can achieve in some of the following ways:

- Using key performance indicators (KPIs) to analyze your strengths and weaknesses
- Regularly reviewing the pricing of your products
- Examining the price elasticity of demand for your products and services
- Frequently timing your discounts and promotions
- Focusing your efforts on the most profitable customers
- Providing premium products

- Charging for the extras you provide
- Winning customer loyalty and intimacy
- Increasing the company brand value in the targeted markets
- Licensing some of your intellectual property
- Developing new product lines
- Finding new market segments
- Negotiating better deals with suppliers
- Making marketing more cost-efficient
- Keeping your product ahead of the competition
- Eliminating product offerings that have low sales and low margins
- Using spare capacity to increase output
- Decreasing inventory

- Assessing your general and administration business costs
- Reviewing your areas of business waste and reducing them
- Maximizing the cost-effectiveness of your fixed assets
- Creating systems, processes and procedures that are not ignored by employees
- Using efficient equipment
- Increasing staff productivity, performance and accountability
- Avoiding unprofitable projects
- Strategizing for continuous improvement

Metrics for Profitability:

- Profit / Customer
- Profit / Employee
- Profit / Customer Visit
- Profit / Tons

- Profit / Revenue
- Profit / R&D Expenses
- Profit / Manufacturing Costs
- Profit / Marketing Expenses
- Profit / Sales Expenses
- Profit / Total Expenses
- Profit / Sales Channel
- Profit / Market Segment
- Profit / Product
- Profit / Units Sold
- Profit / Inventory
- Profit / Accounts Receivable
- Profit / Total Assets
- Profit / Total Equity
- Profit / Shares Outstanding
- Profit / User

Market Positioning and Market Share in Fast-growing Companies

Positioning is a strategic effort to uniquely influence the target audience about the identity of a company and its products or services.

Market positioning involves the following four steps:

Draft a positioning statement: The positioning statement identifies who the company is, what it stands for, who the target customer is, what the customer needs are, and how those specific needs will be addressed. Then it identifies a statement of distinction that sets the brand apart from the competition. Brand Promises are reasons customers buy from you.

Competitor Analysis: Find out your competitor's revenues, market share, return on investment, investment in R&D, strategic partnerships, current objectives, assumptions, capabilities, resources, and strategy. You can positon your product for market fit, functionality, relevance and differentiation. Pricing strategy can be optimized for volume, margin, predictability, long term relationship and/or reputation.

Industry Positioning: Michael Porter's tools are useful for positioning a company in an industry. The five forces that shape the nature of competition are: (1) rivalry among current competitors, (2) threat of new entrants, (3) substitutes and complements, (4) power of suppliers, and (5) power of buyers. They determine the attractiveness of an industry, its profit potential, and the ease and attractiveness of moving from one strategic position to another.

Develop a unique positioning idea: Refine and finalize the positioning statement. Test your positioning idea by gathering information about the planned purchase of your products, from focus groups, surveys, in-depth interviews, ethnography, polls, etc.

A company's **market share** is its sales measured as a percentage of its industry's total revenues. Relative market share is used to compare the company's market share to its largest competitor. Only the market leader has a relative market share of more than 1.

Companies increase market share through innovation, strengthening customer relationships, improving distribution methods, lowering prices, improving quality or functionality, using customer ideas, hiring smartly, being more flexible, and acquiring competitors. Higher market share puts companies at a competitive advantage. Companies with high market share often receive better prices from suppliers, experience greater production, better brand recognition and reduced unit costs. According to Boston Consulting Group, most efforts to increase market share depress profits, at least in the short term. Some companies are happy to ride along the industry growth curve, and may want to take a break from increasing their market share during the coming year.

Portfolio Management of Products and Businesses

The Boston Consulting Group Matrix depicts four quadrants that distinguish high and low markets and a product's position in those markets. The products are grouped as "stars," "cash cows," "dogs," and "question marks." Stars, which are dominant products in a growing market, and cash cows, which are
legacy products that control a steady or diminishing market make up the bulk of profitability for a company. Dogs are low-yielding products in a declining market that drain resources and are contenders for elimination. Product decisions are most difficult around question marks, which are products that have some level of potential for innovation in a market that is growing.

General Electric and McKinsey Consulting expanded and adapted the BCG Matrix to suit its diverse product families and numerous acquisitions. It uses "Industry Attractiveness" and "Business Unit Strength" to anchor its X-Y Matrix. The Low-Medium-High ratings give a broader view of products in order to identify those to develop, markets to expand into, products to re-tool, and products to eliminate.

Scoring and mapping methods, as well as matrix and bubble charts, provide data and visualizations to help make the decisions for effective product portfolio management. You can also add weight to other elements such as experience, common sense, or educated guesses.

Innovation portfolios are not for product innovation alone. They also include process, service, and business model innovation. Many companies also track external innovations in which they have invested, or have options to pick up. Issues such as riskiness, likely benefits, and relevance to different business units, functions or markets are considered.

On average, high-performing firms direct 70% of their innovation resources to enhancements of core offerings, 20% to adjacent opportunities, and 10% to transformational initiatives. But individual firms may deviate from that ratio for sound strategic reasons. A mid-stage technology firm may want to devote 45% to core, 40% to adjacent and 15% to transformational initiatives.

These are the questions you need to answer while managing a portfolio of businesses in a large company: What is the fundamental potential of each business in terms of the markets served, growth, margin, and competitive advantage? What is the value to the company of each business today and what will it be in the future? What is the contribution to share price, market capitalization, and the future valuation multiple? Does the portfolio have an appropriate mix of businesses that offer short-term growth and long-term growth? Are there enough cash-generating businesses to fund growth businesses? Is the portfolio sensibly diversified in terms of business risk? Do the businesses fit the company's investment thesis and style of competition? Are there synergies across them? Can the businesses take advantage of the corporate center's assets or capabilities to create additional value? Is the value of the portfolio, taken as a whole, greater than the sum of the parts? Is the portfolio attractive to desired investors?

Corporate Governance in For-Profit Companies

Corporate governance is the set of mechanisms, processes and relations by which corporations are controlled and directed. The board of directors, executives, shareholders, creditors, auditors and regulators have a say in corporate affairs.

Some of the *Commonsense Principles of Corporate Governance* are:

- Directors should have the skills, experience, time, integrity and expertise necessary to oversee the corporation's business.
- Directors should be willing and able to speak candidly and question the CEO and management.
- The board should be involved in strategic planning, setting aside time to consider long-term strategy regularly.

- The board should take responsibility for succession planning and risk management.
- The board should take an active role in setting executive compensation.
- Investors should exercise their voting rights thoughtfully to create long-term value.

Corporate governance in the United States is marked by activist institutional investors, an open market for corporate control, independent outside directors on the board, long-term equity-based compensation for executives, and gatekeepers who monitor the process of market disclosure.

Corporate Governance in IPO companies:

According to the law firm Davis, Polk and Wardell, in their 2016 survey, they found that 83 per cent of the IPO companies surveyed had a classified board, as opposed to only 10 per cent of the companies in the

S&P 500. Similarly, they found that 97 per cent of IPO companies surveyed had plurality voting as opposed to only 4 per cent of the companies in the S&P 500. Some observations about non-controlled IPOs were that most of them had independent boards, their audit committees were fully independent, they had plurality voting, a classified board, single class common stock, they did not have an independent chairman, and they did not permit shareholder action with written consent. Non-voting shares, staggered boards, plurality voting, etc. are considered to impair shareholder rights.

KPMG interviewed a lot of **Private Company Directors** to find:

- The top three governance challenges include improving risk management oversight, assessing innovation and emerging competition, and establishing company strategy.

- Other key governance challenges for private companies include achieving regulatory compliance, leadership succession planning and global compliance.
- The most visible challenges to board effectiveness include resource constraints, conflicts of interest and a compromised board due to an overrepresentation of controlling shareholders.
- New technologies like Big Date Analytics may be able to get more relevant and efficient reporting for management and the board.
- They want their governance processes and controls to improve M&A or IPO outcomes, mitigate financial risk and improve financial performance.

Corporate Image of an Exit Stage Company

A good corporate image is a genuine asset and it leads to increased revenues and higher corporate valuation. The major elements are:

1. the core business and financial performance of the company
2. the reputation and performance of its brands
3. its reputation for innovation or technological prowess
4. its policies toward its employees
5. its external relations with customers, shareholders, and the community
6. the perceived trends in the markets in which it operates

The single most important factor in the corporate image is a company's core business performance which includes financial results. 59% of investors consider brand strength and market position in their top 5 choices.

Your brand is the emotional, mental and experiential associations your marketplace makes with your company and its offerings. Your market position is the frame of reference through which you want your market to see you. Your investors are not the same as your customers, and they need to be segmented differently.

10 Critical Branding Principles for IPOs

Here are the critical points for a company to think about as it considers going public.

1. Because the IPO market is saturated, the brand needs to communicate something unique and interesting to investors. A company's brand needs to stand out and create a level of excitement and enthusiasm.
2. Develop a robust brand, not just a logo.

3. Investment banks are looking for strong brands with a story to sell through to prospective investors. Help them.
4. Strong brands often attract strong bank partners. Brands like Goldman Sachs, Citi, Merrill Lynch and Morgan Stanley bring credibility and prestige, and they want to align with brands that can succeed over time.
5. Brand strength continues to be viewed as a leading indicator of future financial performance.
6. More than ever, a strong brand can partly overcome investor fears about lack of data.
7. Experienced investors can see through the underwriter's hype but a genuine brand can justify the fanfare and garner a higher price. Build one.
8. Unlike years past, brands today first have to resonate with and be embraced by employees.
9. A strong brand can continue to build momentum for the company during the quiet period.

10. A strong brand adds a rich dimension to the IPO story, beyond the financial fundamentals.

Have a crisis-management plan in place. It is wise to have not only a plan of action ready but also a team prepared to step in to do damage control. Your image is a valuable financial asset and should be protected like any other asset.

Prioritize the communities you want to reach in their order of importance, and budget accordingly. Segment your customers, investors, employees, media, analysts, regulators, business partners, suppliers, and general public, and leverage your spending to communicate with the desired segments.

It can take up to a year to have a measurable brand impact.

If you're in the C-suite you need exposure. You should work with marketing to get your name and face out as a trusted industry leader. This should include corporate blogs, speaking engagements and accessibility to the business press. Your company should produce white papers quoting you. You should speak at industry conferences, participating in industry roundtables and webcasts. When the desired audiences see a CEO active in his/her industry and a thought leader, it gives them more confidence in the company.

Valuation in an Exit Stage Company

When the company is in the scaling stage, investors (venture capital and private equity investors) find companies similar to the investee, and figure out their valuation to revenue ratio, which they call the "multiple". Then they multiply your company's revenues by that multiple to get the valuation. Sometimes, they discount forecasted earnings by the time value of money to get the valuation.

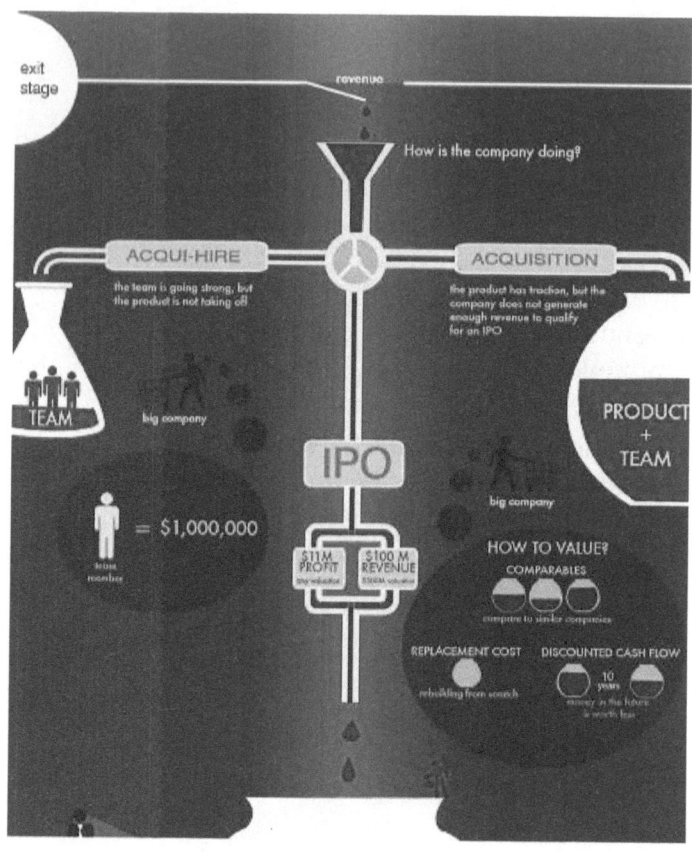

In most cases, the IPO or acquisition does not happen before year 5 of founding the company. Investment Bankers project company growth to determine its valuation before the IPO. They use a balanced perspective of present revenue and promise of growth. The methods used by investment bankers to determine valuation include:

1. Comparable Multiples

   a. Price to Earnings Multiple
   b. Market to Book Value Multiple
   c. Price to Revenue Multiple
   d. Enterprise Value to Earnings Before Interest and Taxes Multiple

2. Discounted Cash Flow

   a. Net Present Value based method
   b. Internal Rate of Return based method
   c. Economic Value Added based method

The Process for an Initial Public Offering in the United States is as follows:

1. Examine the state of the stock market and the potential for an IPO.
2. Interview several investment banks and select two or three. Select a law firm and accounting firm with IPO experience.
3. Draft the registration statement. Prepare the issuer to become a public company.
4. File the registration statement with the SEC. Gain clearance from a stock exchange like the NASDAQ.
5. Revise the registration statement in response to comments from the SEC.
6. Print preliminary prospectus and begin marketing efforts.
7. Conduct "road show" presentations to potential large investors.
8. File final amendment to the registration statement and request the

SEC to declare it effective. Price the offering and start selling your stocks.

Road shows involve the lead underwriters and company executives giving presentations to institutional investors. Determining the appropriate offering price is the most important thing the investment bank can do for your company. If the issue is priced too high, it may be unsuccessful and be withdrawn. If the issue is priced too low, the existing shareholders will experience an opportunity loss. If you have a built your company's reputation, and if you have marketed well to investors, you will have no problem selling your stocks at your IPO.

Pre-IPO Task List

Once you decide that you want to take your company public, you need to find suitable accountants, lawyers and investment bankers. You may want to discuss the IPO process with other publicly traded company CEOs and CFOs.

Two years before the IPO:

- Build the right executive team
- Engage in Strategic Planning
- Establish Financial Accounting and Reporting systems
- Create a Financial Planning and Analysis team
- Add independent members to your Board of Directors
- Create an Audit committee
- Evaluate Corporate Governance practices
- Build a positive public image

- Establish incentive compensation plans
- Start writing Management's Discussion and Analysis statements

Strategic and Financial moves that could enhance the value of your IPO:

- Debt Financing
- Corporate re-organization
- Equity Financing
- Business Alliances and Partnerships
- Mergers and Acquisitions

Important financial IPO success factors:

- Debt to Equity ratio
- EPS growth
- Sales growth
- Return on Equity
- Profitability growth

Important non-financial IPO success factors:

- Management team
- Corporate strategy and Execution
- Brand and Market position
- Operational effectiveness
- Corporate Governance

Table of Contents from a Sample Prospectus

- PROSPECTUS SUMMARY
- RISK FACTORS
- SPECIAL NOTE REGARDING FORWARD-LOOKING STATEMENTS
- USE OF PROCEEDS
- DIVIDEND POLICY
- INDUSTRY AND OTHER DATA
- CAPITALIZATION

- DILUTION
- ▆▆ AND ▆▆ UNAUDITED PRO FORMA CONDENSED COMBINED FINANCIAL INFORMATION
- SELECTED CONSOLIDATED FINANCIAL DATA
- MANAGEMENT'S DISCUSSION AND ANALYSIS OF FINANCIAL CONDITION AND RESULTS OF OPERATIONS
- BUSINESS
- MANAGEMENT
- EXECUTIVE AND DIRECTOR COMPENSATION
- CERTAIN RELATIONSHIPS AND RELATED PERSON TRANSACTIONS
- PRINCIPAL AND SELLING STOCKHOLDERS
- DESCRIPTION OF CAPITAL STOCK
- SHARES ELIGIBLE FOR FUTURE SALE

- MATERIAL U.S. FEDERAL TAX CONSIDERATIONS FOR NON-U.S. HOLDERS OF COMMON STOCK
- UNDERWRITING (CONFLICTS OF INTEREST)
- LEGAL MATTERS
- EXPERTS
- WHERE YOU CAN FIND MORE INFORMATION
- INDEX TO CONSOLIDATED FINANCIAL STATEMENTS

About the Author

Ms. Hetal Shah is an expert in strategy, innovation, entrepreneurship and product management. She has over 10 years of professional work experience in the sales, marketing, operations, administrative and entrepreneurial fields. She has worked in the financial services, philanthropy, technology and management consulting sectors. She has worked for four technology startups in the past. She is knowledgeable about the software and telecommunications industries. She was born in 1972. She attained a bachelor's degree in Civil engineering from Bradley University in 1993. In 2001, she was a founder and CEO of a telecommunications-media startup in Boston. Now, she is a business coach and independent management consultant in Boston. She has lived in the Boston area for over 20 years. She is well-read about business, finance and entrepreneurship. She is looking for artificial intelligence, robotics, software and telecommunications companies as clients for her independent management consulting services. She can be reached at hetaliscoy@yahoo.com.

www.ingramcontent.com/pod-product-compliance
Lightning Source LLC
Chambersburg PA
CBHW031548210526
45464CB00003B/1208

9781977599124